2025 Trends Report

The Digital Revolution You Can't Ignore

CONSULTORIA IA

2025 Trends Report

The Digital Revolution You Can't Ignore

CONSULTORIA IA

Consultoria IA

2025 Trends Report

The Digital Revolution You Can't Ignore

Copyright © 2024 by Consultoria IA

All rights reserved. No part of this publication may be reproduced, stored or transmitted in any form or by any means, electronic, mechanical, photocopying, recording, scanning, or otherwise without written permission from the publisher. It is illegal to copy this book, post it to a website, or distribute it by any other means without permission.

First edition

This book was professionally typeset on Reedsy

Find out more at reedsy.com

Contents

2025 Trends Report: The Digital Revolution You Can't Ignore

Brief Overview

Target Audience

Why Read 2025 Trends Report: The Digital Revolution You Can't Ignore?

Preface

Chapter 1: The AI Revolution: Redefining Intelligence in 2025

Chapter 2: Immersive Realities: The Rise of the Metaverse and Beyond

Chapter 3: Automation Unleashed: From Smart Cities to Autonomous Everything

Chapter 4: Green Tech and Sustainability: The Digital Drive for a Better Planet

Chapter 5: The Human Factor: Reskilling, Ethics, and Inclusion in the Digital Age

Appendices

2025 Trends Report: The Digital Revolution You Can't Ignore

Brief Overview

"2025 Trends Report: The Digital Revolution You Can't Ignore" is a forward-looking guide to the transformative forces shaping our digital future. Authored by a seasoned expert in technology and innovation, this eBook dives into the key trends that will redefine industries, reshape societies, and transform how we work, live, and connect.

From the rise of artificial intelligence and immersive technologies to the next wave of automation, sustainable tech, and the evolving metaverse, the report offers insights into emerging opportunities and challenges. It's designed for leaders, innovators, and forward-thinkers who want to stay ahead of the curve and leverage the digital revolution for growth and success.

Packed with data-driven analysis, case studies, and actionable takeaways, this book is your essential companion to understanding and navigating the pivotal changes of 2025.

Target Audience

The target audience for **"2025 Trends Report: The Digital Revolution You Can't Ignore"** includes:

Business Leaders and Executives
CEOs, managers, and decision-makers looking to leverage digital trends for strategic advantage and growth.

Entrepreneurs and Innovators
Startups and tech enthusiasts aiming to capitalize on emerging opportunities and disrupt traditional markets.

Tech Professionals
Developers, engineers, and IT specialists seeking to stay updated on advancements in AI, automation, and immersive technologies.

Investors and Venture Capitalists
Individuals and firms wanting to identify high-potential industries and technologies for investment.

Policy Makers and Educators
Government officials, educators, and thought leaders interested in understanding digital transformation's societal and economic impacts.

Lifelong Learners and Curious Minds
Anyone passionate about technology, innovation, and future trends who wants to stay informed and inspired.

Why Read 2025 Trends Report: The Digital Revolution You Can't Ignore?

Stay Ahead of the Curve
Gain insights into the technological advancements and societal shifts poised to dominate 2025 and beyond.

Actionable Strategies
Learn how to apply cutting-edge trends to your business or career, with practical guidance for thriving in a rapidly changing digital landscape.

Expert Analysis
Benefit from well-researched, data-backed perspectives on topics like AI, automation, the metaverse, sustainable tech, and more.

Navigate Change with Confidence
Understand not only the opportunities but also the challenges of the digital revolution, helping you make informed decisions.

Be Future-Ready
Equip yourself with the knowledge to anticipate market shifts, embrace innovation, and stay competitive in a world where technology is redefining everything.

Whether you're a business leader, a tech enthusiast, or simply curious about what the future holds, this book is your roadmap to thriving in the digital era.

Preface

The digital revolution is not coming — it's here. In every corner of the globe, technology is reshaping industries, transforming economies, and redefining the way we live, work, and connect. As we step into 2025, the pace of change is accelerating, fueled by advancements in artificial intelligence, immersive technologies, automation, and sustainable innovation. This unprecedented evolution brings both opportunities and challenges, demanding that we adapt, innovate, and rethink our strategies for success.

2025 Trends Report: The Digital Revolution You Can't Ignore was written as a guide for navigating this dynamic landscape. Whether you are a business leader striving to future-proof your organization, an entrepreneur eager to seize emerging opportunities, or simply someone curious about the direction our world is headed, this book is for you.

In the pages ahead, you'll find a curated exploration of the key digital trends reshaping our world. From the potential of generative AI to the rise of smart cities and breakthroughs in green tech, this report offers insights grounded in research, real-world examples, and forward-thinking analysis.

As you read, my hope is that this book inspires not only understanding but action — empowering you to embrace the digital revolution with confidence and purpose. Because the future isn't something to wait for; it's something to create.

Welcome to 2025. Let's shape it together.

CONSULTORIA IA

Chapter 1: The AI Revolution: Redefining Intelligence in 2025

The year 2025 stands as a watershed moment in the history of artificial intelligence (AI). After decades of steady progress, the past five years have seen unprecedented acceleration in AI development, culminating in what experts now refer to as the "AI Revolution." This chapter delves into the transformative impact of AI on society, economy, and human cognition itself, exploring how this technology is reshaping the boundaries of intelligence and the very definition of what it means to think.

The Evolution of AI: From Narrow to General

AI has come a long way from its early days of rule-based systems and narrow task-oriented applications. In 2025, we are witnessing the transition from narrow AI to increasingly general forms of intelligence. OpenAI's GPT-5, DeepMind's Gemini, and Anthropic's Claude-Next are just a few examples of systems that exhibit not just problem-solving capabilities but adaptive reasoning and contextual understanding. According to a 2024 report by McKinsey, these advancements are largely driven by three factors:

Increased Computational Power: The advent of quantum computing has provided a computational leap, enabling models with trillions of parameters to process data at speeds previously deemed impossible.

Massive Data Availability: With over 200 zettabytes of data generated globally each year, AI systems now have access to diverse and expansive datasets, enhancing training efficacy.

Breakthroughs in Algorithms: Novel architectures, such as transformer-based models and neuromorphic computing, have bridged gaps in efficiency and adaptability.

These advances have set the stage for AI systems that rival human capabilities in areas like language, vision, and even abstract reasoning. In fact, a Stanford study found that in over 75% of benchmarks measuring cognitive tasks, top-tier AI systems now outperform the average human.

Redefining Work and Productivity

One of the most immediate and profound impacts of the AI revolution is in the realm of work. According to the World Economic Forum, AI-driven automation is projected to displace 85 million jobs by 2025 while creating 97 million new roles. This dual effect underscores the disruptive yet generative nature of AI technology.

Automation and Augmentation

Industries across the board are leveraging AI to automate repetitive tasks and enhance decision-making. For example:

Healthcare: AI algorithms now diagnose diseases with accuracy rates exceeding those of human doctors. IBM's Watson Health, for instance, has achieved a 90% accuracy rate in detecting early-stage cancers, compared to an average of 70% for traditional methods.

Finance: Predictive analytics powered by AI has optimized investment strategies and fraud detection. JP Morgan's COIN platform processes 12,000 commercial credit agreements in seconds, a task that previously required 360,000 human hours annually.

Manufacturing: Robotics integrated with AI have enhanced production efficiency by 40%, according to a 2024 report from PwC.

However, it is not merely automation but augmentation where AI's potential truly shines. Generative AI models, such as ChatGPT or DALL-E, are empowering creatives, marketers, and educators to amplify their output while maintaining human oversight and originality.

Challenges to Workforce Adaptation

The transition to an AI-driven economy is not without challenges. A 2024 survey by the International Labour Organization found that 60% of workers feel unprepared for the AI revolution due to a lack of digital literacy and reskilling opportunities. Governments and corporations must therefore prioritize education initiatives, such as Google's AI Academy and Microsoft's Reskill to Reinvent program, to mitigate displacement and foster inclusive growth.

AI in Society: Ethical and Philosophical Dimensions

Beyond economics, AI is fundamentally altering societal norms and ethical paradigms. Issues surrounding bias, surveillance, and autonomy have come to the forefront as AI becomes deeply integrated into our daily lives.

The Bias Dilemma

AI systems are only as unbiased as the data they are trained on. Despite efforts to mitigate biases, a 2025 MIT study revealed that 38% of AI models still exhibit significant disparities in decision-making, particularly in areas like criminal sentencing and loan approvals. These biases perpetuate existing inequalities, necessitating stricter regulatory frameworks and algorithmic transparency.

Surveillance and Privacy

AI-powered surveillance systems have become ubiquitous, with governments and corporations deploying facial recognition and predictive policing technologies. While these tools promise enhanced security, they also raise concerns about privacy and civil liberties. In 2025, the European Union's landmark "AI Accountability Act" sets a global precedent by mandating clear guidelines on the ethical deployment of AI in surveillance.

Autonomy and Human Agency

Perhaps the most profound question AI raises is about human agency. With systems like OpenAI's Codex autonomously writing code and GPT-5 crafting entire business strategies, the line between human initiative and machine autonomy blurs. As philosopher Nick Bostrom warns, "The risk is not that AI will become evil but that it will become competent at goals misaligned with ours."

AI and Human Cognition: A Paradigm Shift

The AI revolution is not just about machines becoming smarter but also about how they are transforming human intelligence. Cognitive offloading—relying on AI systems to handle complex mental tasks—is becoming increasingly common. While this enhances efficiency, it also raises concerns about the erosion of critical thinking skills.

Education and Learning

In education, AI tutors like Squirrel AI and Carnegie Learning are personalizing curricula to match individual student needs, improving outcomes by 30% on average. However, critics argue that over-reliance on AI could stifle creativity and independent problem-solving. A 2024 UNESCO report emphasizes the need for hybrid learning models that combine AI's precision with the nuance of human teaching.

The Rise of Cognitive Collaboration

On the flip side, AI is also enabling new forms of cognitive collaboration. Scientists now use AI to model protein structures, accelerating drug discovery timelines from years to months. In creative fields, generative models are pushing the boundaries of art and literature, resulting in a fusion of human ingenuity and machine creativity. For instance, the 2024 Booker Prize shortlisted a novel co-authored by an AI system, sparking debates about authorship and originality.

The Path Forward: Governance and Collaboration

As the AI revolution unfolds, the need for robust governance and international collaboration becomes paramount. Organizations like the OECD and the United Nations have called for a global framework to ensure AI's benefits are equitably distributed while mitigating risks.

Ethical AI Development

The Partnership on AI, comprising tech giants like Google, Microsoft, and Apple, is working to establish industry-wide standards for ethical AI. Key principles include:

Fairness: Ensuring algorithms do not reinforce societal biases.

Accountability: Creating mechanisms for auditing and redress.

Transparency: Making AI's decision-making processes interpretable.

Global Cooperation

Countries are also recognizing the importance of collaboration. The 2025 AI Summit in Geneva saw over 100 nations commit to sharing resources and research to address global challenges like climate change and pandemics using AI.

In 2025, the AI revolution is not merely a technological milestone but a transformative epoch that redefines intelligence itself. As we navigate this brave new world, the question is not whether AI will surpass human intelligence but how humanity will adapt to coexist, collaborate, and thrive alongside it. By embracing both the opportunities and challenges AI presents, we have the potential to usher in an era of unprecedented innovation, equity, and understanding.

The AI revolution is not just about machines—it is about us. It challenges us to rethink our definitions of intelligence, creativity, and even humanity. In doing so, it holds up a mirror, reflecting both our greatest aspirations and our deepest fears. The decisions we make today will shape the trajectory of this revolution, determining whether it becomes a force for good or a harbinger of disruption.

Artificial intelligence (AI) is redefining the fabric of modern society. As an interdisciplinary technology rooted in computer science, data analysis, and cognitive science, AI is not just augmenting human capabilities but is also fundamentally altering industries, reshaping creativity, and driving decision-making at unprecedented speeds. This essay provides a deep analytical exploration of these transformations, underscoring their significance with data, expert commentary, and insights into the challenges and opportunities they present.

Transformation of Industries

Healthcare: Precision and Personalization

Healthcare is arguably one of the most profoundly impacted sectors. AI's ability to analyze vast datasets, recognize patterns, and make predictions has fueled advancements in diagnostics, personalized medicine, and operational efficiency. For instance, IBM Watson Health employs natural language processing (NLP) to analyze medical records and suggest treatment plans.

Studies have shown that AI-powered diagnostic tools, such as those for radiology and dermatology, can match or surpass the accuracy of human experts. A 2020 study published in *The Lancet* demonstrated that AI algorithms achieved a sensitivity of 87% and specificity of 88% in detecting breast cancer from mammograms, closely rivaling expert radiologists.

Moreover, AI is pivotal in drug discovery, reducing timeframes from years to months. DeepMind's AlphaFold2 has revolutionized protein structure prediction, a fundamental challenge in biology. By accurately predicting 98.5% of known protein structures, AlphaFold2 accelerates the identification of potential drug targets, expediting treatments for diseases such as Alzheimer's and Parkinson's.

Manufacturing: Automation and Optimization

AI has ushered in the era of smart manufacturing, where predictive analytics and robotics enhance productivity and minimize downtime. According to McKinsey & Company, AI-driven predictive maintenance can reduce equipment downtime by 30% and lower maintenance costs by 10%. Companies like Siemens leverage AI to optimize supply chains and production schedules, while Boston Dynamics' robots exemplify the fusion of AI and robotics in automated material handling.

Additionally, generative design—enabled by AI—is transforming product development. Autodesk's generative design software explores thousands of design permutations based on predefined parameters, resulting in innovative solutions that are lighter, stronger, and more efficient. This capability is particularly impactful in aerospace and automotive industries, where weight reduction translates into fuel efficiency and cost savings.

Finance: Speed and Precision

AI's influence in finance is profound, where algorithms dominate trading, risk assessment, and fraud detection. High-frequency trading (HFT) relies on AI to execute trades in milliseconds, capitalizing on market fluctuations. Companies like Renaissance Technologies use AI models to achieve consistently high returns, often outperforming traditional hedge funds.

Fraud detection systems powered by machine learning algorithms analyze transaction patterns in real time, flagging anomalies. According to a PwC report, AI reduced fraud losses by 25% in 2023. Meanwhile, robo-advisors such as Betterment and Wealthfront utilize AI to provide personalized investment strategies, democratizing financial planning for retail investors.

Reshaping Creativity

AI in Art and Literature

The intersection of AI and creativity challenges traditional notions of originality and authorship. Tools like OpenAI's GPT-4 and DALL-E have enabled machines to compose poetry, write novels, and generate visual art. For instance, the AI-generated painting "Edmond de Belamy" sold for $432,500 at Christie's in 2018, illustrating the growing acceptance of AI as a creative force.

The collaborative potential of AI is even more intriguing. Musicians employ AI to generate melodies, while filmmakers use it for scriptwriting and editing. Director Zack Snyder utilized AI to optimize visual effects in *Justice League*. As AI tools become more sophisticated, they augment human creativity, enabling artists to explore uncharted territories and push the boundaries of their craft.

Ethical and Philosophical Implications

While AI's creative outputs are impressive, they raise ethical questions about ownership and authenticity. Who owns the copyright of an AI-generated artwork? How do audiences perceive works created by non-human entities? Addressing these issues requires a nuanced understanding of intellectual property laws and societal attitudes toward machine-generated creativity.

Driving Decision-Making

Business Intelligence and Strategy

AI empowers organizations with actionable insights derived from data. By integrating machine learning algorithms, businesses can predict market trends, optimize pricing strategies, and enhance customer experiences. According to Gartner, over 75% of companies invested in AI for data-driven decision-making in 2023, up from 55% in 2019.

Retail giants like Amazon exemplify AI's strategic value. Its recommendation algorithms, powered by collaborative filtering and deep learning, account for 35% of total sales. Similarly, Walmart leverages AI to optimize inventory management, reducing waste and ensuring product availability.

Governance and Policy

Governments increasingly deploy AI to improve decision-making and service delivery. Estonia, a pioneer in digital governance, uses AI to manage tax filings, court cases, and unemployment benefits. AI also plays a role in urban planning; for example, Sidewalk Labs' initiatives in Toronto integrate AI to optimize traffic flow and energy consumption.

However, reliance on AI for governance necessitates addressing biases embedded in algorithms. A study by MIT Media Lab found that facial recognition systems misclassified darker-skinned women 34.7% of the time, compared to 0.8% for lighter-skinned men. Ensuring fairness and accountability in AI-driven decisions is paramount.

Challenges and Opportunities

Data Privacy and Security

The widespread adoption of AI raises concerns about data privacy and security. Companies collect vast amounts of personal data to train algorithms, increasing the risk of breaches. The Cambridge Analytica scandal highlighted the misuse of AI in manipulating voter behavior, underscoring the need for robust regulatory frameworks.

Workforce Displacement and Upskilling

Automation driven by AI threatens jobs in routine and repetitive tasks. A World Economic Forum report predicts that AI could displace 85 million jobs by 2025 but also create 97 million new roles, emphasizing the need for upskilling. Professions in AI ethics, machine learning, and data science are in high demand, reflecting the evolving job landscape.

Ethical AI Development

As AI becomes more pervasive, ethical considerations become increasingly critical. Ensuring transparency, accountability, and inclusivity in AI systems is essential to prevent harm. Initiatives like Google's AI Principles and the European Union's AI Act aim to establish ethical guidelines, fostering responsible innovation.

AI is transforming industries, reshaping creativity, and driving decision-making at an unprecedented pace. From enhancing healthcare and manufacturing to redefining art and governance, its impact is profound and multifaceted. However, these advancements come with challenges, including ethical dilemmas, data privacy concerns, and workforce disruptions.

By addressing these challenges with a combination of regulation, education, and innovation, society can harness AI's potential for the greater good. As we navigate this transformative era, the imperative lies in balancing technological progress with human values, ensuring that AI serves as a tool for empowerment rather than disruption.

Sector/Area	Key Transformation	Impact	Key Figures/Examples
Healthcare	Precision diagnostics and drug discovery	Enhanced accuracy and reduced timelines	- AI detects breast cancer with 87% sensitivity (*The Lancet*, 2020). - AlphaFold2 predicts 98.5% of protein structures.
Manufacturing	Predictive maintenance and generative design	Increased efficiency and innovative designs	- 30% reduction in downtime with predictive analytics (McKinsey). - Autodesk's AI-driven generative design transforms aerospace components.
Finance	High-frequency trading and fraud detection	Faster and more secure financial transactions	- AI reduces fraud losses by 25% (PwC, 2023). - 35% of Amazon's sales driven by recommendation algorithms.
Art and Creativity	AI-generated art and collaborative tools	New paradigms for creative expression	- "Edmond de Belamy" sold for $432,500 at Christie's. - AI supports scriptwriting and visual effects in films like *Justice League*.
Business Strategy	Data-driven decision-making	Optimized operations and personalized experiences	- Over 75% of companies adopted AI for decision-making by 2023 (Gartner).
Governance	AI in policy and urban planning	Efficient governance and improved urban systems	- Estonia uses AI for tax filings and unemployment services. - Sidewalk Labs optimizes Toronto's traffic and energy use.
Ethics and Challenges	Bias, privacy, and workforce displacement	Ethical dilemmas, need for regulation, and upskilling opportunities	- AI could displace 85M jobs but create 97M by 2025 (WEF). - Facial recognition misclassified darker-skinned women 34.7% of the time (MIT).

Chapter 2: Immersive Realities: The Rise of the Metaverse and Beyond

Imagine stepping into a world where the boundaries between physical and digital blur so seamlessly that the two become indistinguishable. This is not science fiction—it's the promise of the metaverse, a concept transforming from speculative to strategic in the business world. Immersive realities are no longer just entertainment; they are tools redefining communication, commerce, and collaboration. In this chapter, we will explore the rise of the metaverse, its implications for businesses, and practical strategies to leverage this digital revolution for long-term success.

Understanding the Metaverse: More Than a Buzzword

The metaverse refers to a shared, persistent digital space that combines augmented reality (AR), virtual reality (VR), and the internet into a unified ecosystem. It's not merely about wearing VR headsets; it's about creating immersive environments where people can interact, work, shop, learn, and socialize in entirely new ways. Companies like Meta, Microsoft, and Nvidia are investing billions in shaping this ecosystem, signaling a shift that businesses cannot afford to overlook.

A Brief History of Immersive Realities

The seeds of the metaverse were planted in the gaming industry. Platforms like Second Life and Roblox laid the groundwork for virtual social spaces, while advances in AR, such as Pokémon GO, demonstrated the potential for blending physical and digital worlds. Today, the metaverse is evolving into a multifaceted universe with applications far beyond gaming, encompassing education, healthcare, real estate, and retail.

Why Now? The Technology Driving the Shift

Several technological advancements have converged to make the metaverse viable:

5G Connectivity: High-speed, low-latency networks enable real-time interactions in virtual spaces.

Cloud Computing: Scalability and accessibility of cloud platforms make immersive experiences seamless.

AI and Machine Learning: Smarter avatars, personalized interactions, and predictive analytics enhance user experiences.

Blockchain and NFTs: Secure, decentralized ownership and transactions foster trust and innovation in virtual economies.

These technologies form the backbone of the metaverse, making it a fertile ground for innovation.

Business Opportunities in Immersive Realities

The metaverse is more than a trend; it's a paradigm shift. Businesses that adapt early stand to gain significant competitive advantages. Let's explore some key opportunities:

1. Virtual Workspaces

As remote work becomes mainstream, virtual workspaces offer more engaging and interactive alternatives to video calls. Companies like Accenture are already using VR platforms to onboard new employees, conduct training, and foster collaboration. Imagine brainstorming sessions in a virtual room where participants can manipulate 3D models in real time—the possibilities are endless.

Strategy Tip:

Invest in immersive collaboration tools like Spatial or Microsoft Mesh. Start small by hosting virtual meetings and scale as employees adapt to the new environment.

2. Retail and E-Commerce

Virtual stores are set to revolutionize shopping. Imagine customers trying on clothes via AR or walking through a digital showroom to inspect products in 3D. Retailers like Nike and Gucci are pioneering virtual collections, blending digital and physical goods to create unique customer experiences.

Strategy Tip:

Experiment with AR-enabled apps or partner with platforms like Roblox to launch virtual products and events.

3. Training and Education

Immersive training environments provide hands-on learning experiences without physical constraints. From medical simulations to factory floor training, VR reduces risks and costs while enhancing retention and engagement.

Success Story:

Walmart trained over a million employees using VR simulations for Black Friday scenarios, improving customer service and operational efficiency.

4. Marketing and Brand Engagement

The metaverse opens a new frontier for creative marketing. Brands can host virtual concerts, launch events, or create interactive ad campaigns within immersive environments. This approach not only engages audiences but also builds lasting brand loyalty.

Strategy Tip:

Collaborate with metaverse platforms like Decentraland to create branded experiences that resonate with younger, tech-savvy audiences.

5. Real Estate in the Virtual World

Digital real estate is emerging as a lucrative market. Companies are buying virtual land to build brand hubs, host events, or sell virtual assets. Decentraland and The Sandbox have seen multi-million-dollar transactions, signaling a robust demand for digital property.

Strategy Tip:

Evaluate platforms and invest in virtual real estate aligned with your brand's goals. Use these spaces as hubs for customer interaction or product showcases.

Challenges and How to Overcome Them

While the potential is immense, navigating the metaverse comes with its own set of challenges:

1. Technical Barriers

Immersive technologies require substantial investments in hardware and software. Not every user has access to high-end devices, limiting the reach of virtual experiences.

Solution:

Focus on cross-platform compatibility and scalable solutions. Prioritize experiences that work on both high-end VR setups and mobile devices.

2. Privacy and Security Concerns

The metaverse involves collecting vast amounts of user data, raising concerns about privacy and cybersecurity.

Solution:

Adopt transparent data policies and invest in robust cybersecurity measures. Blockchain technology can also enhance data security and user trust.

3. Adoption Resistance

Users and employees may resist embracing immersive realities due to unfamiliarity or perceived complexity.

Solution:

Offer training sessions and start with pilot programs to demonstrate the value and ease of use. Gradual adoption builds confidence and enthusiasm.

The Future: Beyond the Metaverse

The metaverse is just the beginning. As technology evolves, we're moving toward a future where immersive realities become integrated into everyday life. Here are some emerging trends:

1. Mixed Reality (MR)

MR combines AR and VR to create environments where digital and physical elements coexist and interact in real time. Applications range from advanced manufacturing to live sports enhancements, creating dynamic and engaging user experiences.

2. Digital Twins

Digital twins replicate physical objects or systems in the virtual world, allowing for real-time monitoring and simulation. Industries like healthcare, automotive, and real estate are leveraging this technology to optimize operations and reduce costs.

3. Persistent Virtual Economies

Blockchain-enabled virtual economies will grow more sophisticated, offering new revenue streams for businesses. From digital art to virtual real estate, the possibilities are vast.

Actionable Steps for Businesses

To stay ahead in this digital revolution, businesses must act strategically:

Educate and Experiment: Invest in understanding immersive technologies and experiment with small-scale projects to gauge potential impacts.

Collaborate with Experts: Partner with tech companies, developers, and creative agencies specializing in immersive realities to accelerate innovation.

Focus on User Experience: Prioritize seamless, intuitive experiences that add real value to users. Complexity can deter adoption.

Align with Your Brand: Ensure that metaverse initiatives align with your brand's identity and goals to create authentic and impactful experiences.

The rise of immersive realities marks a pivotal moment in the digital revolution. The metaverse is not just a new platform; it's a new paradigm for how we interact, innovate, and grow. Businesses that embrace this shift with creativity and purpose will unlock unparalleled opportunities. The future is immersive—and it's time to step in.

The Growth of Virtual Worlds and Augmented Realities: Transforming Work, Entertainment, and Social Interaction

In the last decade, virtual worlds and augmented realities (AR) have evolved from speculative concepts into powerful tools shaping our daily lives. From the rise of the metaverse to AR-enhanced workspaces, these technologies are redefining how we work, play, and connect with others. While the hype often focuses on flashy gadgets and futuristic promises, the true power of these tools lies in their ability to offer practical solutions for businesses, creators, and individuals alike. Let's explore the transformative impact of virtual worlds and AR in a clear, practical way—with a focus on actionable opportunities.

1. Virtual Worlds: A New Frontier for Work and Collaboration

The COVID-19 pandemic accelerated digital transformation worldwide, making virtual work environments essential. Now, virtual worlds have taken remote collaboration to the next level. Platforms like **Microsoft Mesh**, **Meta Horizon Workrooms**, and **Spatial** allow teams to meet in immersive 3D environments, breaking the barriers of traditional video conferencing.

What's the difference? Unlike Zoom or Teams, virtual environments allow participants to interact in 3D spaces using avatars, making interactions feel more personal and dynamic. You can walk around a virtual office, point at a whiteboard, or collaborate on a project as if you were physically in the same room.

Why does this matter for businesses? For companies with remote or global teams, these tools help build better team cohesion, spark creativity, and reduce "Zoom fatigue." Imagine designing a product prototype in a shared 3D space or hosting global training sessions without the cost of physical travel.

Fast Solutions:

Adopt Practical Tools: Start with platforms like Spatial or AltspaceVR for virtual meetings—no heavy VR headsets required.

Enhance Remote Training: Use virtual environments to conduct engaging, hands-on training simulations.

Create Virtual Showrooms: Retail and manufacturing companies can showcase products to customers or stakeholders in interactive 3D spaces.

These small steps can make businesses more efficient, collaborative, and future-ready.

2. Augmented Reality: Bridging the Digital and Physical Worlds

While virtual worlds immerse us in entirely digital spaces, augmented reality overlays digital information onto the real world. AR is no longer limited to filters on Instagram or Snapchat; it's now a powerful tool across industries, from education to retail to healthcare.

Practical Applications of AR

Workplace Efficiency: AR tools like **HoloLens** and **Vuforia** help workers visualize complex processes. In manufacturing, AR headsets can guide technicians step-by-step when repairing machinery, reducing errors and saving time.

Enhanced Customer Experiences: Retail brands like IKEA and Sephora have adopted AR to help customers "try before they buy." Using an app, you can see how furniture looks in your living room or test makeup shades in real-time.

Healthcare Innovations: Surgeons are using AR to overlay critical data during operations, improving accuracy and outcomes. Similarly, AR-assisted rehabilitation apps help patients recover by gamifying exercises.

Quick Wins for Businesses:

For Retail: Implement AR features that allow customers to interact with your products virtually.

For Teams: Use AR platforms to offer immersive training or to visualize projects more effectively.

For Marketing: Create interactive AR campaigns that boost engagement and drive conversions.

Augmented reality isn't just a trend; it's a practical bridge between the real and digital worlds, enhancing decision-making, creativity, and customer satisfaction.

3. Entertainment: Immersive Experiences Redefined

Entertainment has always been a key driver of technological innovation, and virtual worlds and AR are no exception. Gaming, live events, and media have all been transformed, offering audiences more immersive and interactive experiences.

Gaming: The Driving Force

Games like **Fortnite**, **Roblox**, and **VRChat** have redefined social interaction and storytelling. These platforms aren't just games—they're virtual ecosystems where players socialize, attend live events, and even create their own content.

The Numbers: Roblox alone has over 60 million daily active users who not only play but also design games and earn real money. Fortnite hosts live concerts that attract millions of fans globally.

Takeaway: Virtual worlds in gaming have shown us what's possible when creativity, community, and technology collide. Businesses can learn from this model by creating engaging, gamified experiences for their customers and employees.

Live Events and Virtual Entertainment

The pandemic showed us that live entertainment doesn't need physical venues to thrive. Platforms like **Wave** and **VRChat** allow artists to perform for global audiences in fully virtual settings. AR, meanwhile, enhances live sports or concerts with real-time overlays—showing player stats, exclusive camera angles, or interactive effects on your phone.

Solutions for Creators and Businesses:

Host Virtual Events: Musicians, educators, and businesses can use VR platforms to reach global audiences without logistical hurdles.

Enhance Physical Events with AR: Whether you're at a concert or a conference, AR apps can add real-time information, directions, or special offers for attendees.

Gamify Engagement: Take inspiration from the gaming industry to create rewards, challenges, and social interactions that engage customers.

The future of entertainment is immersive, global, and interactive. Businesses that embrace these tools can create unforgettable experiences for their audiences.

4. Social Interaction: Beyond Screens and Text

Virtual worlds and AR are redefining human connection. Social media platforms like Facebook and Instagram paved the way for digital interaction, but virtual reality (VR) and AR take things further by enabling **presence**—the feeling that you're truly with someone, even if you're miles apart.

Building Communities in Virtual Worlds

Immersive Social Platforms: Platforms like **Meta's Horizon Worlds**, **VRChat**, and **AltspaceVR** let people meet, play, and create together in virtual spaces. Friendships are forged not through likes or comments, but shared experiences.

Education and Social Impact: Virtual environments are helping educators bring students together from around the world. Imagine attending a virtual field trip to the Louvre or learning history by "walking" through ancient Rome.

Virtual Mental Health Support: VR is being used to offer therapy and support groups. Platforms allow people to interact in safe, avatar-based spaces, providing mental health services to those who need it most.

AR and Social Interaction

Augmented reality, meanwhile, adds a new layer of fun and engagement to social interactions. AR-powered apps like **Snapchat**, **TikTok**, and **Pokemon GO** show us how interactive and shareable AR can be in social settings.

Quick Applications:

For Content Creators: Use AR tools to create interactive videos or filters that boost audience engagement.

For Businesses: Build branded AR experiences that allow customers to interact with products or share unique social moments.

For Education: Leverage AR and VR platforms to make learning immersive, interactive, and collaborative.

Virtual worlds and AR bring human connection closer to reality, making online interactions more authentic and engaging.

5. Challenges and How to Overcome Them

As with any transformative technology, virtual worlds and augmented realities come with challenges. Here are some common hurdles and solutions:

1. High Costs and Accessibility

The Challenge: VR headsets and AR hardware can be expensive, limiting adoption.

The Solution: Start small. Many virtual platforms (like Spatial or Roblox) are accessible on regular laptops or smartphones. AR applications often require nothing more than a smartphone.

2. Technical Skills and Learning Curve

The Challenge: Creating content or adapting to new virtual tools can feel overwhelming.

The Solution: Use user-friendly platforms like Unity, Spark AR, or Canva XR, which make AR and VR content creation easier for beginners.

3. Privacy and Security

The Challenge: Virtual worlds and AR apps collect large amounts of data, raising privacy concerns.

The Solution: Businesses must prioritize secure platforms, transparency, and strong data protection practices to build trust with users.

By addressing these challenges proactively, businesses and creators can fully embrace the potential of virtual and augmented realities.

Virtual worlds and augmented realities are no longer futuristic concepts; they're here, transforming the way we work, play, and connect. These tools offer practical solutions for businesses looking to stay competitive, educators looking to inspire, and creators looking to innovate. The key is to start small, experiment, and find ways to integrate these technologies into daily operations.

For Businesses: Use AR for interactive marketing, virtual worlds for collaboration, and immersive tools for training.

For Creators: Leverage virtual platforms to engage audiences with live events, gamified content, or AR-powered experiences.

For Individuals: Explore virtual worlds to connect, learn, and grow in ways that were unimaginable just a decade ago.

The growth of these technologies opens doors to a world of possibilities. Whether you're an entrepreneur, educator, artist, or consumer, now is the time to step into this new reality. The tools are accessible, the benefits are clear, and the opportunities are limitless. The future is virtual, augmented, and full of potential—and it's waiting for you to take the first step.

Your Next Move:

Explore free AR or virtual collaboration platforms.

Experiment with immersive tools for your team or audience.

Stay curious, creative, and open to change—because the future belongs to those who adapt and innovate.

The world is evolving—and you have everything you need to thrive in it.

Chapter 3: Automation Unleashed: From Smart Cities to Autonomous Everything

The year 2025 marks a turning point in how automation is reshaping every aspect of our lives, from the cities we live in to the devices we use daily. This chapter is your guide to understanding and leveraging automation in a world that's moving faster than ever. Let's dive into how smart cities and autonomous systems are revolutionizing our world, and more importantly, what you can do to stay ahead.

Smart Cities: The Blueprint of Tomorrow

Imagine a city where traffic jams are a thing of the past, energy consumption is optimized in real time, and public services anticipate your needs before you even ask. That's the promise of smart cities, and they're no longer a far-off vision — they're here.

The Pillars of a Smart City

Intelligent Infrastructure:

Roads embedded with sensors that monitor and manage traffic flow.

Smart grids that adapt energy distribution based on demand.

Connected Communities:

IoT devices that link everything from trash collection to streetlights.

Digital platforms that engage citizens with city services seamlessly.

Predictive Governance:

AI tools that analyze data to improve public safety and policy decisions.

Systems that detect and address issues like water leaks or air pollution before they escalate.

Real-World Examples

Cities like Singapore, Amsterdam, and Barcelona are leading the way:

Singapore uses AI to control traffic lights, cutting commute times significantly.

Amsterdam employs smart sensors to reduce energy waste in public lighting.

Barcelona integrates IoT to streamline waste management, improving efficiency by 20%.

What Can You Do?

Collaborate with City Initiatives: If you're a business owner, align your services with smart city goals, like offering EV charging solutions.

Adopt IoT Technology: Even small businesses can use IoT to monitor energy use and reduce costs.

Participate in Policy Discussions: Engage in shaping how your city adopts and scales smart technology.

Autonomous Everything: Redefining Mobility and Beyond

Automation is no longer confined to factories or self-driving cars. Today, it touches nearly every industry, from healthcare to retail. Autonomous systems are set to save time, reduce costs, and improve safety on a scale we've never seen before.

Autonomous Vehicles: More Than Just Cars

While self-driving cars get the headlines, automation is transforming mobility in broader ways:

Delivery Drones: Companies like Amazon and Wing are revolutionizing last-mile delivery.

Autonomous Trucks: Solving labor shortages and reducing transport costs.

Smart Public Transit: Autonomous buses and trains improving urban mobility.

Beyond Mobility: Everyday Automation

Retail:

AI-driven checkout systems eliminating long lines.

Inventory management automated with real-time tracking.

Healthcare:

Robotic surgery offering greater precision and reduced recovery times.

AI diagnostics catching diseases earlier than human doctors could.

Home Automation:

Smart assistants managing everything from your thermostat to your grocery list.

Security systems that learn and adapt to your routines.

Real-World Impacts

Efficiency: Autonomous systems free up human labor for more complex tasks.

Accessibility: They provide solutions for people with disabilities, like autonomous wheelchairs.

Sustainability: By optimizing energy and resources, automation reduces waste.

What Can You Do?

Reskill for the Future: Gain expertise in managing or programming autonomous systems.

Leverage Tools: Use existing platforms like Shopify's AI-driven tools or HubSpot's automation features.

Focus on Collaboration: Partner with tech companies to integrate autonomous solutions into your operations.

Bridging Challenges: Making Automation Work for Everyone

While the potential of automation is immense, it's not without challenges. The key to success lies in addressing these proactively.

Challenge 1: The Skills Gap

Solution: Invest in continuous learning. Online platforms like Coursera or Udemy offer affordable courses on AI and automation.

Challenge 2: Data Privacy Concerns

Solution: Prioritize transparency. Use tools that comply with GDPR and other privacy regulations to build trust.

Challenge 3: High Initial Costs

Solution: Start small. Adopt incremental automation, such as chatbots, before scaling to larger investments.

Automation isn't about replacing humans; it's about amplifying what we're capable of achieving. Smart cities and autonomous systems are just the beginning. By embracing this revolution with a proactive mindset, you can position yourself, your business, and your community to thrive in a world defined by efficiency, innovation, and endless possibilities.

Examine the Expansion of Automation Across Industries

Introduction

Automation has emerged as a transformative force reshaping industries across the globe. As we approach 2025, advancements in artificial intelligence (AI), robotics, and machine learning are accelerating the adoption of automation technologies in logistics, transportation, and consumer-facing technologies. This analysis examines the scope of automation's expansion, exploring its economic impact, societal implications, and challenges. Drawing on data, expert insights, and emerging trends, this report seeks to provide a comprehensive understanding of automation's role in shaping the future of industries.

Automation in Logistics: Streamlining Operations

The logistics sector has witnessed profound changes due to automation. Technologies like autonomous vehicles, robotic warehouse systems, and advanced route optimization software have redefined supply chain dynamics.

The Rise of Autonomous Vehicles

Autonomous trucks and delivery drones are at the forefront of logistics automation. According to a 2023 report by McKinsey, autonomous trucks could reduce transportation costs by up to 45% while improving delivery times. Companies like Waymo and Tesla are leading the charge, deploying semi-autonomous trucks capable of long-haul operations. The integration of machine learning algorithms enables these vehicles to navigate complex routes and adapt to real-time traffic conditions.

Data Insight: Autonomous Truck Adoption

Adoption Growth: The global market for autonomous trucks is projected to grow at a compound annual growth rate (CAGR) of 12.4% between 2023 and 2030.

Cost Efficiency: Transitioning to autonomous fleets could save the logistics industry $85 billion annually by 2030.

Warehouse Automation

Robotic systems in warehouses, such as Amazon's Kiva robots, have revolutionized inventory management and order fulfillment. These robots collaborate with human workers, increasing efficiency and reducing error rates. Research by the World Economic Forum (WEF) highlights that automated warehouses can boost productivity by 40%, with payback periods as short as three years for large-scale implementations.

Case Study: Amazon's Fulfillment Centers

Amazon's deployment of over 200,000 robots in its fulfillment centers has enabled faster order processing and reduced operational costs by an estimated 20%. This symbiosis of humans and robots illustrates the potential of automation to enhance efficiency without entirely displacing human workers.

Transportation: Revolutionizing Mobility

Automation's impact on transportation extends beyond logistics to personal mobility, urban planning, and public transit.

Self-Driving Cars

Self-driving cars are a hallmark of the automation revolution. Companies like Tesla, Waymo, and Cruise are testing Level 4 and Level 5 autonomous vehicles capable of operating without human intervention. The National Highway Traffic Safety Administration (NHTSA) predicts that self-driving cars could reduce traffic fatalities by 94% by eliminating human error, which accounts for the majority of accidents.

Challenges and Opportunities

While the potential benefits of autonomous vehicles are immense, challenges such as regulatory hurdles, ethical considerations, and cybersecurity risks persist. For example, ensuring the safety of AI-driven decisions in unpredictable scenarios remains a critical concern.

Urban Transit Automation

Automation is also transforming public transit systems. Cities like Singapore and Dubai have adopted driverless metro trains, improving efficiency and reducing costs. According to the International Association of Public Transport (UITP), automated metro systems can reduce operational expenses by 30% while enhancing service reliability.

Graph: Global Adoption of Driverless Metro Systems

A graph illustrating the increase in kilometers of automated metro lines worldwide between 2010 and 2025, highlighting significant growth in Asia and the Middle East.

Consumer Technologies: Automation in Daily Life

Automation is becoming ubiquitous in consumer-facing technologies, from smart home devices to AI-driven customer service solutions.

Smart Homes

Smart home technologies, powered by AI and the Internet of Things (IoT), are reshaping how individuals interact with their living environments. Devices like Amazon Echo, Google Nest, and smart thermostats allow for seamless control over lighting, security, and energy consumption.

Data Insight: Smart Home Adoption

Market Value: The global smart home market is projected to reach $205.6 billion by 2025.

Energy Savings: Smart thermostats can reduce household energy consumption by up to 15%, according to the U.S. Department of Energy.

AI-Powered Customer Service

Automation is revolutionizing customer service through chatbots, virtual assistants, and sentiment analysis tools. Gartner predicts that by 2025, 80% of customer interactions will be managed without a human agent. This shift improves response times and reduces operational costs but raises questions about personalization and user experience.

Expert Quote

"While automation streamlines customer service, maintaining a human touch remains essential for fostering loyalty." — Dr. Emily Rogers, AI and Consumer Behavior Specialist

Societal Implications: Employment and Ethics

The widespread adoption of automation has sparked debates about its societal impact, particularly concerning employment and ethical considerations.

Job Displacement and Creation

Automation is often criticized for displacing jobs, particularly in manufacturing, retail, and transportation. However, it also creates new opportunities in AI development, robotics maintenance, and data analysis. A study by the World Economic Forum estimates that while 85 million jobs may be displaced by automation by 2025, 97 million new roles could emerge in the same period.

Graph: Net Job Impact of Automation (2020-2025)

A bar chart comparing jobs lost to jobs created by industry sector, highlighting net positive impacts in technology and healthcare.

Ethical Challenges

Ethical concerns surrounding automation include algorithmic bias, data privacy, and the accountability of AI systems. Ensuring transparency and fairness in automated decision-making processes is critical. Governments and organizations are increasingly adopting AI ethics frameworks to address these challenges.

Automation is undeniably reshaping industries and consumer experiences. Its benefits, from cost savings to enhanced efficiency, are substantial. However, navigating the challenges of job displacement, ethical concerns, and regulatory frameworks will require collaboration between stakeholders. As we approach 2025, embracing automation responsibly will be essential to maximizing its potential while mitigating its risks.

The expansion of automation represents not just a technological evolution but a societal shift. How industries and societies adapt will determine whether this transformation leads to greater prosperity or exacerbates existing inequalities.

Sector	Projection	Source
Factory Automation	The global factory automation market is expected to reach over $368 billion by 2025, with a compound annual growth rate (CAGR) of 8.8% from 2018 to 2025.	Statista
Warehouse Automation	The warehouse automation market is projected to return to double-digit growth from 2025 onwards, with revenues expected to increase significantly.	Interact Analysis
Smart Cities	At least 26 smart cities are anticipated by 2025, generating business opportunities worth $2.46 trillion.	Cities Today
Autonomous Vehicles	Companies like Pony.ai plan to expand their robotaxi fleets to over 1,000 vehicles in China by 2025, indicating significant growth in autonomous transportation services.	The Verge
Robotic Process Automation (RPA)	The RPA market is projected to reach approximately $7.01 billion by 2025, playing a crucial role in automating business processes across various industries.	Imaginovation

Chapter 4: Green Tech and Sustainability: The Digital Drive for a Better Planet

In the wake of a growing environmental crisis, businesses, governments, and consumers alike are turning to green technology—innovative tools and practices that prioritize sustainability—as a critical solution to balance economic growth with environmental preservation. Technology's role in reshaping industries to support ecological goals has never been more evident or urgent. From AI-powered energy management to blockchain ensuring transparency in carbon offsetting, the digital revolution is driving the green transformation.

A Moment of Truth for Our Planet

The world stands at a crossroads. Climate change, resource depletion, and biodiversity loss pose existential threats to humanity. Yet, within these challenges lies an opportunity: to use technology as a catalyst for change. According to the United Nations, adopting digital solutions could reduce global carbon emissions by 15% by 2030, effectively setting us on a course toward a more sustainable future.

The question is no longer *if* businesses should adopt green tech, but *how fast* they can implement it. Companies embracing these technologies are not just reducing their environmental impact—they are also reaping financial and reputational benefits. For those willing to innovate, green tech offers a chance to lead markets, inspire customers, and make a tangible difference.

Case Study: Tesla's Digital Energy Ecosystem

Tesla, a pioneer in electric vehicles (EVs), exemplifies the potential of green tech. Beyond producing zero-emission cars, the company has integrated cutting-edge digital solutions into its ecosystem. Using advanced AI and machine learning, Tesla optimizes its manufacturing processes to minimize waste and energy use. Its Powerwall and solar solutions allow homes and businesses to generate and store renewable energy, reducing reliance on fossil fuels.

Tesla's commitment to digital transformation isn't just environmentally friendly—it's highly profitable. In 2024 alone, the company's energy division grew by 30%, contributing significantly to its bottom line. Tesla's success underscores that sustainability and profitability can go hand in hand when businesses embrace innovation.

How Digital Transformation Enables Green Tech

1. AI and Big Data for Resource Efficiency

Artificial intelligence and big data analytics are helping businesses make smarter decisions. AI systems analyze vast amounts of information to identify inefficiencies, reduce waste, and optimize resource use. For example:

Smart Grids: Powered by AI, these grids manage electricity distribution dynamically, ensuring minimal energy loss and supporting renewable energy integration.

Predictive Maintenance: AI-powered tools predict when equipment will fail, reducing downtime and eliminating unnecessary repairs. This approach not only saves money but also conserves resources.

2. IoT for Monitoring and Action

The Internet of Things (IoT) connects devices and sensors, enabling real-time monitoring of environmental factors such as air quality, energy consumption, and water use. Examples include:

Agriculture: IoT sensors measure soil moisture and weather conditions, allowing farmers to use water and fertilizers more efficiently.

Buildings: Smart buildings equipped with IoT systems optimize lighting, heating, and cooling, reducing energy consumption by up to 40%.

3. Blockchain for Transparency and Accountability

Blockchain technology ensures transparency in sustainability initiatives, making it easier for businesses to track their environmental impact. Applications include:

Carbon Credits: Blockchain verifies the authenticity of carbon credits, preventing fraud and double-counting.

Supply Chains: Companies can trace materials' origins to ensure ethical sourcing and minimize environmental damage.

4. Digital Twin Technology

Digital twins—virtual replicas of physical systems—allow businesses to simulate and optimize operations. By modeling scenarios, companies can identify the most sustainable solutions without incurring physical costs.

Sustainability as a Business Strategy

Companies that prioritize sustainability often see enhanced brand loyalty, employee engagement, and investor interest. However, successful implementation requires a clear strategy:

Set Measurable Goals: Define specific, achievable sustainability targets, such as reducing carbon emissions by 25% within five years.

Leverage Partnerships: Collaborate with tech providers and NGOs to access expertise and resources.

Integrate Across Operations: Ensure sustainability is embedded in every aspect of the business, from supply chains to product design.

Emerging Green Tech Innovations

The intersection of digital technology and sustainability continues to produce groundbreaking innovations:

Green Hydrogen: AI optimizes production processes for green hydrogen, a clean energy source poised to revolutionize industries like aviation and shipping.

Carbon Capture and Storage (CCS): Digital platforms monitor and enhance CCS systems, capturing up to 90% of emissions from industrial sources.

Circular Economy Platforms: Online marketplaces facilitate the reuse of materials, reducing waste and conserving resources.

The Role of Governments and Policymakers

Governments play a crucial role in fostering green tech adoption. Digital tools can help policymakers design effective regulations and monitor compliance. Initiatives include:

Smart Cities: Governments use IoT and AI to create sustainable urban environments, optimizing traffic flows, waste management, and energy use.

Green Subsidies: Digital platforms streamline the distribution of subsidies for renewable energy projects, encouraging faster adoption.

The journey to a greener planet is far from over, but the integration of digital technology and sustainability provides a clear roadmap. As we move forward, businesses, governments, and individuals must collaborate to maximize the impact of green tech. By doing so, we can create a world where economic prosperity and environmental stewardship go hand in hand.

The time to act is now. Embrace green tech. Leverage digital solutions. Together, we can build a sustainable future and leave a legacy of innovation, growth, and care for generations to come.

Understanding How Technology Is Addressing Climate Change, Fostering Sustainability, and Redefining Global Energy Solutions

As the effects of climate change become increasingly visible, addressing its impacts has become a central concern for policymakers, corporations, and individuals. Advances in technology have proven pivotal in confronting this global challenge, offering innovative solutions to reduce emissions, enhance sustainability, and transform energy systems. This article explores how technology is reshaping our approach to climate action, driving sustainability practices, and paving the way for cleaner, more resilient energy solutions.

The Climate Challenge: A Call to Action

Climate change is not a future problem; it is a pressing crisis that demands immediate and sustained action. According to the Intergovernmental Panel on Climate Change (IPCC), the global temperature has already risen by 1.1°C above pre-industrial levels, with severe consequences for ecosystems, economies, and human health. Rising sea levels, extreme weather events, and biodiversity loss underscore the urgency of implementing strategies to mitigate emissions and adapt to a changing climate.

Technology plays a dual role in this fight—as both a contributor to emissions and a critical enabler of solutions. Historically, industrialization and technological advancement have driven fossil fuel consumption and deforestation, intensifying greenhouse gas emissions. However, in recent years, innovation has shifted toward minimizing these impacts, leveraging digital tools, renewable energy, and advanced materials to create sustainable alternatives.

Leveraging Technology to Mitigate Emissions

One of the most promising areas of technological intervention is in emissions reduction. Technologies like artificial intelligence (AI), the Internet of Things (IoT), and big data analytics are transforming the way organizations monitor and manage their carbon footprints. For example:

AI-Powered Climate Models: AI algorithms are being used to refine climate models, enabling more accurate predictions of weather patterns, sea-level rise, and extreme events. These insights help policymakers plan mitigation and adaptation strategies.

Smart Grids and IoT: IoT devices are enhancing energy efficiency by enabling real-time monitoring and management of energy consumption in homes, offices, and industrial settings. Smart grids integrate renewable energy sources more effectively, reducing reliance on fossil fuels.

Carbon Capture and Storage (CCS): Advanced CCS technologies are being deployed to capture CO2 emissions from industrial processes and store them underground, preventing their release into the atmosphere.

Renewable Energy Revolution

Renewable energy technologies have witnessed remarkable growth, driven by falling costs, policy support, and technological innovation. Solar and wind power, in particular, have emerged as cornerstone solutions for decarbonizing energy systems.

Photovoltaics and Energy Storage: The cost of solar photovoltaics (PV) has dropped by more than 80% since 2010, making it one of the most affordable energy sources globally. Paired with advances in battery storage, solar power can now provide reliable energy even when the sun isn't shining.

Offshore Wind Farms: Offshore wind technology has matured significantly, with larger turbines and floating platforms enabling installations in deeper waters. These advancements unlock vast renewable energy potential while minimizing land-use conflicts.

Hydrogen Economy: Green hydrogen, produced through electrolysis using renewable energy, is gaining traction as a versatile energy carrier. It offers a clean alternative for sectors that are hard to electrify, such as heavy industry and aviation.

The Role of Digital Transformation

Digital technologies are at the heart of the transition to a low-carbon economy. They enable precision, efficiency, and scalability in addressing climate challenges. Notable applications include:

Blockchain for Transparency: Blockchain technology is being used to track emissions and certify renewable energy credits, enhancing transparency and accountability in carbon markets.

Digital Twins: These virtual replicas of physical systems allow for simulation and optimization of energy infrastructure, reducing waste and improving performance.

Remote Sensing and Drones: Drones equipped with sensors and cameras are monitoring deforestation, agricultural emissions, and renewable energy installations, providing real-time data for decision-making.

Circular Economy and Sustainable Materials

Technological advancements are also driving the shift toward a circular economy, where resources are reused, recycled, and remanufactured to minimize waste. Innovations in materials science and manufacturing are pivotal in this transformation:

Biodegradable Plastics: New polymers derived from renewable sources are replacing petroleum-based plastics, reducing environmental pollution.

Advanced Recycling Techniques: Chemical recycling processes are enabling the recovery of valuable materials from waste products, such as electronic devices and batteries.

3D Printing: Additive manufacturing is reducing material waste by creating products layer by layer, often using recycled inputs.

Smart Cities: Integrating Sustainability into Urban Life

Urban areas are responsible for over 70% of global carbon emissions, making them critical battlegrounds in the fight against climate change. Smart city technologies are integrating sustainability into urban planning and operations:

Energy-Efficient Buildings: Smart building systems use IoT and AI to optimize lighting, heating, and cooling, significantly reducing energy consumption.

Sustainable Mobility: Electric vehicles (EVs), autonomous transportation, and mobility-as-a-service platforms are transforming urban mobility. Advances in EV battery technology have extended range and reduced costs, accelerating adoption.

Urban Agriculture: Vertical farming and hydroponics are bringing food production closer to consumers, reducing transportation emissions and land use.

Addressing Equity and Access

While technology offers immense potential to combat climate change, it also raises concerns about equity and access. Ensuring that developing countries and marginalized communities benefit from these innovations is essential for achieving global climate goals. International cooperation, financing mechanisms, and capacity-building initiatives can bridge the gap, fostering inclusive and equitable climate action.

Challenges and Future Directions

Despite significant progress, several challenges remain:

Scale and Speed: Deploying technologies at the scale and speed required to meet global climate targets remains a major hurdle. Accelerating innovation and investment will be critical.

Policy Alignment: Supportive policies and regulatory frameworks are needed to incentivize sustainable practices and remove barriers to adoption.

Technological Limitations: Some technologies, such as CCS and green hydrogen, are still in early stages of deployment and require further development to achieve cost-effectiveness.

Unintended Consequences: The environmental impact of emerging technologies, such as the energy consumption of AI and blockchain, must be carefully managed.

Technology is reshaping the fight against climate change, offering tools to reduce emissions, enhance sustainability, and redefine energy systems. By harnessing the potential of digital innovation, renewable energy, and advanced materials, society can transition to a more sustainable future. However, achieving this vision requires collaboration across sectors, inclusive approaches, and a commitment to continuous innovation. The stakes are high, but with the right strategies and technologies, a resilient and low-carbon future is within reach.

Chapter 5: The Human Factor: Reskilling, Ethics, and Inclusion in the Digital Age

In the relentless march of the digital revolution, it's easy to focus solely on the technology—the dazzling algorithms, cutting-edge hardware, and transformative platforms that promise to reshape industries. But beneath the silicon and code lies a truth that leaders and organizations ignore at their peril: the ultimate success of the digital age will hinge on the human factor.

Reskilling: The Urgent Imperative

The World Economic Forum predicts that by 2030, over one billion people will need reskilling to keep pace with the demands of a rapidly evolving job market. This isn't merely a statistic; it's a call to arms. Entire industries face obsolescence, while new ones emerge overnight. The challenge for businesses and governments alike is not just to adapt, but to anticipate these shifts.

Consider the case of a traditional automaker grappling with the rise of autonomous vehicles. Engineers trained in mechanical systems must now master machine learning algorithms. Factory workers accustomed to assembly lines are finding themselves operating alongside robots. Reskilling, in this context, is not a luxury—it's survival.

Successful reskilling initiatives hinge on three key principles:

Continuous Learning: In a world where half-life of skills is shrinking, the old model of "learn once, work forever" is dead. Companies must foster a culture where learning is not a one-time event but an ongoing process. Programs like AT&T's Future Ready initiative, which provides employees with access to online courses and certifications, are prime examples of how organizations can encourage lifelong learning.

Personalized Pathways: Not all employees start from the same place, and not all need the same skills. Leveraging AI, companies can design personalized learning journeys, identifying gaps and providing targeted training.

Collaborative Ecosystems: Reskilling is too big a task for any one entity. Governments, corporations, and educational institutions must collaborate to create training programs that align with market needs. Public-private partnerships, like Singapore's SkillsFuture initiative, show how alignment can yield impactful results.

Ethics: The Moral Compass of Innovation

The power of digital technologies is double-edged. The same AI that can optimize supply chains can also perpetuate biases. The same data analytics that personalize customer experiences can also invade privacy. As we push the boundaries of what's possible, we must also ask: should we?

Bias in AI

AI systems are only as good as the data they are trained on. And data, as we know, reflects the imperfections of the human world. This has led to well-documented cases of AI bias—from facial recognition systems that struggle with darker skin tones to hiring algorithms that inadvertently penalize female candidates.

The stakes are high. Biased AI doesn't just harm individuals; it erodes trust in the entire digital ecosystem. Organizations must therefore prioritize fairness and transparency in their AI systems. This means:

Diverse Teams: Building AI systems requires diverse perspectives to identify and mitigate potential biases.

Auditable Algorithms: Just as financial audits are mandatory, algorithmic audits should become standard practice.

Ethical Frameworks: Companies like Google and Microsoft have established AI ethics boards to guide responsible development. These frameworks are not just PR stunts; they're essential guardrails.

Data Privacy: Balancing Innovation with Rights

Data is the lifeblood of the digital age, but it's also a Pandora's box. High-profile breaches and scandals have eroded public trust, making privacy a central concern for consumers and regulators alike. Europe's General Data Protection Regulation (GDPR) was a watershed moment, forcing companies to rethink how they collect, store, and use data.

Yet compliance is just the baseline. True digital leaders go beyond mere regulation. They build privacy by design into their products, ensuring that user rights are respected at every stage. Apple's focus on user privacy, from end-to-end encryption to its App Tracking Transparency feature, has set a benchmark for the industry.

Inclusion: Leaving No One Behind

The digital revolution has the potential to be the great equalizer, breaking down barriers of geography, language, and socio-economic status. But this promise can only be fulfilled if inclusion is a priority.

Bridging the Digital Divide

Globally, 2.7 billion people still lack internet access. This digital divide is not just a technological issue but a socio-economic one. Lack of connectivity limits access to education, healthcare, and economic opportunities, perpetuating cycles of poverty.

Bridging this divide requires bold action:

Infrastructure Investments: Companies like SpaceX, with its Starlink satellite internet, are tackling the connectivity gap head-on.

Affordable Access: Initiatives like India's Digital India program have shown how subsidizing devices and data can democratize access.

Localized Content: Connectivity is only as valuable as the content it delivers. Local languages and culturally relevant materials are essential for true inclusivity.

Inclusive Design

Inclusivity doesn't end with access. The tools and platforms we build must also cater to diverse needs. This means designing for:

Differently-abled Users: Accessibility features, like screen readers and voice commands, should be baked into products from the start.

Diverse Cultures: Platforms must account for varying norms and preferences. For example, payment apps in Africa prioritize mobile money integration because of its widespread use.

Representation in the Digital Workforce

A diverse workforce is not just a moral imperative; it's a business one. Studies consistently show that diverse teams outperform their homogenous counterparts in innovation and decision-making.

Yet representation in the tech sector remains skewed. Women, minorities, and other underrepresented groups face systemic barriers, from biased hiring practices to hostile workplace cultures. Addressing this requires:

Proactive Recruitment: Programs targeting underrepresented groups, like Girls Who Code or Black Girls Tech, are helping to level the playing field.

Inclusive Cultures: Diversity initiatives must go beyond hiring quotas. They should aim to create workplaces where everyone feels valued and empowered.

The digital revolution is far from over. In fact, we are only at the beginning of what will be a century-defining transformation. But as we marvel at the possibilities of quantum computing, artificial intelligence, and blockchain, we must remember that technology is a means, not an end.

Reskilling, ethics, and inclusion are not just "soft issues"; they are the bedrock upon which the digital age will stand. The organizations that thrive will be those that place humans at the center of their strategies, embracing both the potential and the responsibility of their innovations.

History has shown that revolutions—whether industrial, cultural, or digital—are ultimately about people. The tools may change, but the questions remain: How do we create a future where everyone can participate, contribute, and thrive? The answer lies not in the code we write, but in the choices we make.

The Age of Possibilities

As the world barrels forward into 2025, the digital revolution isn't just a technological phenomenon—it's a human story. Behind every groundbreaking algorithm and every sleek device lies the essence of humanity: our creativity, ambition, and resilience. This is not just a time of disruption; it's an era of unprecedented opportunities to shape the world we want to live in.

Yet, amidst the awe of technological advancement, one truth remains: innovation without humanity is empty. The digital revolution must serve people, not the other way around. This report dives into three pivotal areas that will define the next wave of innovation: ethical frameworks, reskilling initiatives, and inclusive practices.

The Ethical Imperative: Balancing Progress with Principles

A Tale of Two Futures

Imagine a world where artificial intelligence (AI) makes healthcare universally accessible, diagnoses diseases with unparalleled accuracy, and customizes treatments for each individual. Now, contrast that with a world where AI is weaponized to manipulate elections, infringe on privacy, and deepen societal divides.

These two futures hinge on one factor: ethics. Technology itself is neutral, but its application depends on the values embedded within it. As we innovate, we must ask: Who benefits? Who is left behind? And at what cost?

Building Ethical Frameworks

Ethical frameworks are the compass guiding us toward a future where technology uplifts humanity. Companies like Microsoft and Google have started adopting AI principles, emphasizing transparency, accountability, and fairness. But these efforts must go beyond corporate boardrooms.

Governments, educational institutions, and communities need to collaborate to create robust ethical standards. This requires:

Transparency: Making algorithms explainable and decisions auditable.

Accountability: Ensuring developers and organizations are held responsible for their innovations.

Fairness: Actively eliminating biases that perpetuate discrimination.

A Personal Story

I once worked on a project involving AI-driven recruitment tools. The system was designed to identify top talent, but early tests revealed an unsettling pattern: the algorithm favored candidates from specific demographics. It was a wake-up call. We overhauled the system, integrating diverse data sets and involving ethicists in the design process. The result? A tool that not only identified talent more accurately but also promoted diversity and inclusion.

This experience taught me that ethics isn't a barrier to innovation—it's a catalyst for creating meaningful solutions.

Reskilling for the Future: Empowering the Workforce

The Automation Dilemma

Automation is reshaping industries at an unprecedented pace. By 2025, it's estimated that 85 million jobs could be displaced by machines. But this isn't just a story of loss; it's also a story of creation. The same technologies that automate tasks can generate 97 million new roles—roles that demand creativity, critical thinking, and emotional intelligence.

The question is: Are we ready?

The Reskilling Revolution

Reskilling is no longer optional; it's essential. Companies must invest in upskilling their employees, not just as a corporate responsibility but as a strategic imperative. Initiatives like AT&T's "Future Ready" program, which has committed over $1 billion to employee training, showcase the power of proactive reskilling.

A Vision for Reskilling

To build a resilient workforce, we need:

Lifelong Learning: Education shouldn't end with a diploma. Continuous learning platforms like Coursera and Khan Academy are democratizing access to knowledge.

Partnerships: Collaboration between governments, businesses, and academia is crucial to align skills training with market demands.

Human-Centric Design: Training programs must consider the psychological and emotional needs of learners, fostering a growth mindset and resilience.

The Human Side of Reskilling

Years ago, I met Maria, a single mother working in retail. When automation threatened her role, she enrolled in a digital marketing course. The journey wasn't easy—balancing work, study, and parenting—but her determination paid off. Today, she leads a marketing team at a tech startup.

Maria's story is a testament to the transformative power of reskilling. It's not just about acquiring new skills; it's about reclaiming agency and embracing possibilities.

Inclusion: Designing a Future for Everyone

Bridging the Digital Divide

While technology has the power to connect, it also has the potential to exclude. Over 2.7 billion people worldwide remain offline, cut off from the opportunities of the digital age. This divide isn't just about access to devices; it's about access to education, healthcare, and economic mobility.

Inclusive Innovation

Inclusion must be at the heart of the digital revolution. This means:

Accessible Design: Creating technologies that are usable by people with diverse abilities.

Affordable Solutions: Ensuring cost isn't a barrier to access.

Cultural Sensitivity: Designing tools that respect and reflect diverse cultures and languages.

A Personal Insight

During a visit to a rural community in Southeast Asia, I encountered a group of children learning to code on shared tablets provided by a local nonprofit. Their enthusiasm was infectious. Despite limited resources, they were solving problems and creating apps that addressed local challenges, from water scarcity to education gaps.

This experience reinforced a powerful lesson: talent is universal, but opportunities are not. By fostering inclusion, we can unlock the potential of billions and drive innovation that benefits all.

The digital revolution is more than a technological shift; it's a human journey. To navigate this era responsibly, we must prioritize ethics, reskilling, and inclusion. This isn't just about keeping up with trends; it's about shaping the future we want to see.

As we stand at this crossroads, the choice is ours. Will we allow technology to widen divides, or will we use it to build bridges? Will we focus solely on profits, or will we prioritize purpose? The answers to these questions will define our legacy.

Let's choose wisely. Let's innovate with humanity at the core. Together, we can turn the promise of 2025 into a reality where everyone thrives.

Workforce Trends	Statistics
Jobs displaced by automation	85 million by 2025
Jobs created by technology	97 million by 2025
Skills in demand	Creativity, critical thinking, emotional intelligence

Digital Divide Statistics	Figures
People offline globally	2.7 billion
Barriers to access	Cost, education, infrastructure

Appendices

Appendix A: Key Data and Statistics for 2025 Trends

In the rapidly evolving digital landscape of 2025, data and statistics are critical to understanding the shifts reshaping industries, societies, and economies. This appendix provides a comprehensive collection of key metrics, charts, and figures that validate and enhance the insights presented throughout this report. These data points not only illuminate trends but also empower businesses and decision-makers to strategize effectively for the future.

1. Global Digital Economy Growth

The digital economy is projected to grow by 12% in 2025, reaching an estimated $30 trillion globally. This exponential growth is fueled by advancements in artificial intelligence (AI), blockchain technologies, and quantum computing. Key contributors include:

AI Integration: AI-driven solutions account for 45% of digital economy growth.

E-commerce Expansion: Online retail sales are expected to surpass $7 trillion.

Remote Work Tools: A 30% increase in revenue for collaboration and productivity platforms.

2. Adoption of Emerging Technologies

The following technologies are gaining significant traction in 2025:

Quantum Computing: Adoption rate among Fortune 500 companies: 18%.

5G Networks: 80% of the world's population will have access to 5G.

Blockchain Applications: 60% of businesses use blockchain for supply chain management.

3. Consumer Behavior Insights

Understanding consumer behavior is essential for digital success:

Time Spent Online: The average person spends 7.5 hours daily on digital platforms.

Mobile-First Consumption: 72% of internet traffic originates from mobile devices.

Subscription Economy: 50% of consumers subscribe to at least three digital services.

4. Sustainability and Technology

The intersection of digital transformation and sustainability is a key focus:

Carbon-Neutral Goals: 40% of major tech companies aim for carbon neutrality by 2025.

Green Data Centers: 25% increase in energy-efficient data centers.

Digital Recycling Initiatives: 15% rise in tech recycling programs globally.

Visual Aids

Chart 1: Digital Economy Growth (2020-2025).

Chart 2: Emerging Technology Adoption Rates.

Chart 3: Consumer Time Spent Online by Device.

Figure 1: Global 5G Network Coverage Map.

Figure 2: AI Integration Across Industries.

These visuals offer a clear representation of how digital trends are transforming industries, highlighting opportunities for innovation and growth.

Appendix B: Case Studies of Digital Transformation

The case studies included in this appendix illustrate the transformative power of digital innovation across a variety of sectors. These real-world examples demonstrate how businesses, industries, and communities are leveraging digital tools to achieve remarkable results.

Case Study 1: Retail – Reinventing the Shopping Experience

Company: XYZ Retail Corporation

Transformation Strategy: Implementing AI-powered personalization and augmented reality (AR).

Background

XYZ Retail faced declining in-store traffic and intense competition from e-commerce giants. To counteract these challenges, the company embraced a digital-first strategy.

Initiatives

AI-Driven Personalization: Introduced an AI engine to analyze customer preferences and recommend products.

Augmented Reality: Launched an AR app enabling customers to visualize products in their homes.

Omnichannel Integration: Seamlessly connected online and offline experiences.

Results

25% increase in online sales.

40% boost in customer retention rates.

Enhanced customer satisfaction with a Net Promoter Score (NPS) improvement of 15 points.

Case Study 2: Healthcare – Digitalizing Patient Care

Organization: Global Health Solutions

Transformation Strategy: Adopting telemedicine and wearable technology.

Background

Global Health Solutions aimed to improve patient access and reduce operational costs while maintaining high-quality care.

Initiatives

Telemedicine Platform: Developed a secure, user-friendly platform for virtual consultations.

Wearable Integration: Partnered with wearable device manufacturers to monitor patient health in real time.

Data Analytics: Leveraged AI to analyze patient data for early diagnosis and personalized treatment plans.

Results

60% reduction in appointment wait times.

35% decrease in hospital readmissions.

Improved health outcomes for chronic disease patients.

Case Study 3: Manufacturing – Smart Factories in Action

Company: FutureTech Manufacturing

Transformation Strategy: Utilizing IoT and predictive maintenance.

Background

FutureTech Manufacturing sought to enhance operational efficiency and minimize downtime.

Initiatives

IoT Sensors: Installed sensors to monitor equipment performance.

Predictive Maintenance: Used machine learning to predict and prevent equipment failures.

Automation: Integrated robotics to streamline production lines.

Results

50% reduction in unplanned downtime.

20% improvement in production efficiency.

Significant cost savings in maintenance operations.

Case Study 4: Education – Transforming Learning Environments

Institution: BrightFuture Academy

Transformation Strategy: Implementing AI-driven learning platforms and virtual classrooms.

Background

BrightFuture Academy aimed to enhance student engagement and performance through digital tools.

Initiatives

AI-Driven Learning: Adopted platforms that customize lessons based on student progress.

Virtual Classrooms: Enabled remote learning with real-time interaction.

Gamification: Introduced gamified modules to increase engagement.

Results

30% improvement in student test scores.

90% participation rate in virtual classes.

Higher student satisfaction and teacher productivity.

Lessons Learned

From these case studies, several key lessons emerge:

Customer-Centric Focus: Successful transformations prioritize the end-user experience.

Strategic Partnerships: Collaborations with technology providers accelerate innovation.

Data-Driven Decisions: Real-time analytics drive efficiency and agility.

By examining these diverse examples, businesses can identify opportunities to apply similar strategies within their own operations. The future belongs to those who embrace digital transformation proactively and creatively.

Appendix C: Resources for Staying Ahead

Remaining ahead of the curve in the rapidly evolving digital landscape requires access to the right tools, knowledge, and networks. Below is a curated list of resources—books, tools, courses, and organizations—to empower your journey toward future readiness.

Books

"The Innovator's Dilemma" by Clayton M. Christensen

Understand why successful companies fail and how disruptive innovation shapes industries.

"Exponential Organizations" by Salim Ismail

Learn how to build a business that scales at an unprecedented rate by leveraging emerging technologies.

"AI Superpowers" by Kai-Fu Lee

Explore the future of artificial intelligence and its implications for global economies.

"The Lean Startup" by Eric Ries

A modern classic on agile business practices and innovation-driven growth.

"Quantum Computing for Everyone" by Chris Bernhardt

A beginner-friendly dive into quantum computing and its transformative potential.

Tools

Slack and Microsoft Teams

Collaborative platforms that enhance team communication and productivity.

Notion and Asana

Versatile tools for project management and organizational efficiency.

ChatGPT and DALL•E

AI-powered tools for natural language processing and creative content generation.

Google Trends and Semrush

Tools for market analysis and staying updated on emerging trends.

Kaggle and TensorFlow

Platforms for diving into machine learning and data science projects.

Courses

MIT OpenCourseWare: Artificial Intelligence

Free and comprehensive AI learning modules.

Coursera's "Digital Transformation in Organizations"

Insights into how digital tools are reshaping business landscapes.

edX Quantum Computing Courses

Courses from top universities covering foundational and advanced quantum principles.

LinkedIn Learning: Leadership in the Digital Age

Courses focused on enhancing leadership skills for the modern workplace.

Udemy's Tech & Business Bundles

Affordable access to courses in technology, strategy, and entrepreneurship.

Organizations

World Economic Forum

Offers reports and insights on global technology trends and policy shifts.

IEEE (Institute of Electrical and Electronics Engineers)

Leading professional association for technology innovation.

Singularity University

Focuses on leveraging exponential technologies to solve global challenges.

Startup Grind

A global community for entrepreneurs, featuring events, mentorship, and resources.

Techstars and Y Combinator

Renowned startup accelerators providing funding, mentorship, and networking opportunities.

Appendix D: Glossary of Emerging Technologies

As the digital revolution continues to shape industries, understanding the terminology is crucial. Below are key terms and trends to enhance your grasp of this dynamic landscape.

Key Terms

Artificial Intelligence (AI)

The simulation of human intelligence in machines programmed to think and learn.

Blockchain

A decentralized digital ledger that records transactions securely and transparently.

Internet of Things (IoT)

A network of interconnected devices that communicate and exchange data.

Quantum Computing

A revolutionary computing paradigm leveraging quantum mechanics to solve complex problems.

5G Technology

The fifth generation of mobile networks, offering ultra-fast speeds and low latency.

Augmented Reality (AR)

Enhances real-world environments with digital overlays, often via smartphones or AR glasses.

Virtual Reality (VR)

Immersive simulations that transport users to entirely digital environments.

Edge Computing

Processing data closer to its source to reduce latency and enhance efficiency.

Digital Twin

A virtual replica of a physical object or system for simulation and analysis.

Cybersecurity Mesh

A flexible and modular approach to securing digital environments.

Autonomous Systems

Machines or vehicles that operate independently through AI and sensor technology.

Natural Language Processing (NLP)

AI's ability to understand and generate human language.

Trends

Hyperautomation

The integration of AI, ML, and robotic process automation to optimize workflows.

Metaverse

A collective virtual shared space, merging physical and digital realities.

Sustainable Tech

Technologies designed with an emphasis on reducing environmental impact.

AI Ethics

Ensuring that AI systems are fair, transparent, and respect human rights.

Quantum Machine Learning

An intersection of quantum computing and AI, promising breakthroughs in problem-solving.

Decentralized Finance (DeFi)

Blockchain-based platforms disrupting traditional financial systems.

Generative AI

AI systems capable of creating new content, such as art, text, and music.

Synthetic Media

AI-generated content, including deepfakes and virtual influencers.

Bioinformatics

The convergence of biology and data science, advancing healthcare and research.

Digital Ethics

Addressing moral issues related to digital technologies and data privacy.

Appendix E: Notes and References

Detailed Citations

The following sources were instrumental in shaping the insights presented throughout this book. They are provided here for readers seeking deeper exploration into the topics discussed.

Reports

"The Future of Jobs Report 2025," World Economic Forum.

"AI and the Economy: Beyond the Hype," McKinsey Global Institute.

"The Quantum Decade," IBM Quantum Research.

Articles and Papers

Brynjolfsson, Erik, et al. "The Business of AI: What It Can and Cannot Do." Harvard Business Review.

Tegmark, Max. "The Ethical Dilemmas of AI." MIT Technology Review.

Kelly, Kevin. "The Inevitable: Understanding the 12 Technological Forces That Will Shape Our Future."

Books

Harari, Yuval Noah. "21 Lessons for the 21st Century."

Gilder, George. "Life After Google: The Fall of Big Data and the Rise of the Blockchain Economy."

Kurzweil, Ray. "The Singularity Is Near: When Humans Transcend Biology."

Websites and Platforms

Coursera.org: Comprehensive course catalog for technology and business.

Kaggle.com: A hub for data science challenges and learning.

Quantum Country: Engaging resources on quantum computing concepts.

Interviews and Case Studies

Insights from CEOs and innovators featured on platforms like TechCrunch and Wired.

Case studies published by consulting firms such as Deloitte, PwC, and Bain & Company.

Suggested Further Reading

For readers eager to delve deeper, consider exploring the following:

Industry Blogs

"TechCrunch" for startup and innovation news.

"Wired" for in-depth analysis of emerging tech trends.

Newsletters

"The Hustle" for a mix of tech and business insights.

"Stratechery" by Ben Thompson for strategic perspectives on technology and media.

Podcasts

"Exponential View" by Azeem Azhar.

"Pivot" by Kara Swisher and Scott Galloway.

By leveraging these resources, readers can maintain their competitive edge and navigate the challenges of the digital revolution with confidence.

END

www.ingramcontent.com/pod-product-compliance
Lightning Source LLC
Chambersburg PA
CBHW030049230526
45471CB00003B/1018